AF412299

Bloodletting

poetry of

Julie Noterman

EcoCultural Perspectives
Phoenix, Arizona

Table of Contents

**Part III
Face the Wind**

Forward

As we listen to the stories that others share with us, we find mirrors: we see our own faces in a reflection. As we search through family photographs, we behold the images of ourselves in continuing transition. In these records of growing up, from child to adult, what do we find? Do we like what we see? Do we remember the joys and pain? What do we remember and what did we forget? The riddle that is asked of all of us: do we ever learn the meaning of our own lives?

Julie Noterman's poetry shares with us that period of her life when she was passing through the doors of change and growth. The poetry of "Bloodletting" is a series of very intense personal reflections and confessions of her visions, relationships and the increasing awareness of her own identity, strengths, and vulnerabilities. Her poetry is the book of her soul as it asked questions and sought answers.

"I write to the praise of God and of man," Dylan Thomas said, and the poems of "Bloodletting" are of that same raw stuff. Resonant with the dreams, hopes and realities that we all share, in the poetry of Julie Noterman we experience that mirror of ourselves, a life akin to our own.

Through all art, we experience the lives and hearts of others; we live for small moments in their worlds. In "Bloodletting" we find ourselves in the cosmos of a young woman full of vision - an eye and a heart looking both inwardly and out. "If the doors of perception were cleansed," wrote William Blake, "we would see things clearly as they truly are." This poetry of Julie Noterman is one step of cleansing, as is all true poetry, for herself and for us. What we do once our eyes are open is the next step.

Stephen M. Barnes

♥

Part I

Bound in Remorse

The Big City

Indeed, she is bound in remorse.

Arching bridges
Spanning skyscrapers
        of artful construct,
Glaze the imagination,
not the appetite.

Such sentiments raw are
too coarse to be swallowed whole.

Still I perform my task
to live day-by-day,
        in exquisite graceful motion,
    a dance to obedience,
        a primal consideration.

However, I will balk
when pushed to perform.
Watch.
Out pops a smile, not meant to beguile,
        to serve as steel girders,
        smeared red like misapplied lipstick,
        for sturdy support.

        Then I will dance
                    dance
                    dance
        endlessly in vacuous peace.
No one need ever know,
least of all, me.

Moving to the Big City

Cutting the corners,
    surviving the day,
    stopping at red lights,
    polite in some ways.
The flash is the same,
    if you enter into the pain
    impossible to wile away.

If you have not been born of the earth,
    you can never embrace its depths,
    hardly reveal its secrets.
You will not see,
    that what you seek will only
    be always everywhere
    around you in plain sight.

I have changed.
How about you?

Where are you among the
    power structures,
    towers rising high
    into the sky?

Beings scurry helter-skelter
    Choked and whiplashed,
    boldly squeezed into dominion.
There is still man.
    How about woman, the good and right?
    Can't see them anywhere within sight.

On Being Left Behind

I am just another woman slipping
through your fingers.
Your finely tapered touch weaves smooth
undulating curves
        connecting the dots of pores in
        my body as I pass through.

Your soft lulling voice
gives rise to wild incantations
scattering the lines
throughout my body
twisting and contorting them
into one internal mass.
        You invite me over.
        I decline.

I decline knowing you will not
permit me an instant
To grasp your fingers and pull up alongside.
        You won't even allow contact.

Because afterwards no trace
of me will remain,
not even a glowing spark that refuses to be
shaken from your fingers.
        I know,
        all flows through by the sway
                of your hands.

Haven't Gotten Around

It was a kind of nothingness.
They all come and go
in small blocks of confusion.

So many men, so easy to get around
and wrap them into small blocks
with their mannerisms,
gestures and facial expressions.

I know from their first word
to the proper reply on my part.
I know especially their weaknesses,
how to capture them, like finding a splinter
jutting out from a velvety piece of wood.

I see a defect to gouge out, to turn into a
smooth curve or sometimes
I dig down deeper inside to find
a cavity of decay, dark and moist,
partially digested organic matter,
that's never been revealed on the outside.
Now I know it's there,
I can scrape it out, one piece at a time,
revealing the crumbling and gnawed wood
you really are, when you speak otherwise.

Haven't gotten around to you yet.
You, who baffle with bursts of unexplainable
actions and quirks.
You can be so beautiful,
then a total bastard.

A Poem

A poem is a prayer
An expression
A likeness of everything
      I perceive,
       receive,
       conceive.

Words to be dispersed
In a manner of style
      deception to one
      comrades to another
Depending on your point of view.

Poems are not always written
And preserved on fragile leaves
Rather lived in moments of
      Interacting
       smiles,
       graces,
       joys,
       pleasures
       and misconceptions.

Dried Flowers

Rescind a romance.
Unravel a rhyme.
Cast away a dead flower
done in delicate time.

Perhaps that harmony
was not meant to be mine.

Bloodletting

I drag my ragged fingernail
Straight down to the small of your back
Parting layers of flesh.
Freeing bloodthirsty droplets
that ooze out in silent unison
to trickle down, a spinal pool.
Pause a numb moment before your quick twist
flings streams through the air
running down your side,
tumbling off drop by drop with a martyred
air, knowing that tomorrow's maid
will only slowly
shake her head at the sight,
stubborn darkened stains,
splotches on the crumpled white sheets.

Love in a Crush-Proof Purse Pack

I want to be your baby doll
wash away your woes
lock you in my bedroom
take away your clothes
then who knows.

I'll open my purse
hide away the key
make sure the door stays closed
so I can make love to you
two weeks in a row.

I look up from my pillow as
you stroll into my bedroom
carrying red roses on a golden platter.
You say you are a servant of art,
a bearer of miracles,
this man who wears diamonds
set in a row.

I say, Open your shirt.
He pulls his arms out of the sleeves,
stands there revealed
and sits down beside me.

I ask all others to leave.

Living in the City

Do not speak so softly
I can't hear you above
the cacophony in the streets.
It's not the roar of buses and cars,
mechanical sounds I hear
ringing in my ears.

It's the pain of the vacuum imprisoned in my
skull that cannot find comfort.

It's the fear of being propositioned for sex
when I walk down the street.
It's the mistrust of hearing the doorbell
ringing late at night.
It's the bats that fly around in my bedroom in
the darkest night.

The desperation feeds my mind
deflates my spirit
goads my body,
by now too numb to respond.

Expect to be easily overtaken by compulsions,
actions to reassure my existence:
I eat to feel my stomach full,
        bombard the taste buds.
I talk just to hear my voice,
        words spoken to be
        broken out of time.
I fuck to exercise the genitalia,
        to feel the warmth generated inside.

I can say I'm alive. I close my eyes.
I will survive and thrive,
blood coursing through my veins.
I carry myself high and follow in stride.

But I hear whispers trailing me
perpetually,
I see clouds that evoke fantasy.
I pray my chants discover a friendly air
current.
       Thoughts
       Dissipate,
       Emaciate,
       Emasculate.
Flowers blossom awhile,
then wither and die, die, die,
into a forever ephemeral form.
       Come, let's now rise and dine
       toast with a chalice of wine.
Bread crumbs catch in your facial hairs.
Your eyes glaze over with alacrity.

Hurry, hurry or you won't be mine.

Lady Luck

Lady of luck
Lady of pleasure
Lady wearing the pearls
Lady with the smile
Lady with the curls

Lady who fucks
Lady of leisure
Lady who fears
Lady who charms
Lady of tears

Lady of love
Lady of treasure
Lady of the years
Lady most certain
She hasn't any peers.

I Live On

If I start from the beginning,
get out the illness,
then I can forget malaise ever existed.
I won't live according to morbid
events of the past.
I'm supposed to be happy,
not as serious as I am.

It just happened.

The little girl dropped her illusions
one by one
pebbles into the stream
round smooth stones once lodged in the
bottom mud then washed ashore.
All fantasies to be forsaken,
overruled, torn apart,
pebbles shaped into teardrops.

Now the river bed is cracked like dry porcelain
for the raindrops ceased to fall, ceased to wash
over her eyes.
Now prowlers rummage through
garbage cans,
        knock them over clattering,
        contents scatter,
        beer cans and all.

Some days I want to cut off an arm,
some days greater
vengeance is in order.
Vacillate between
        murder and suicide.

However, the thoughts are
too vague to be taken
seriously by anyone, even me.

But I perform them anyway at night in my bed
wishing you were here, solely to satisfy my
inner desires, only to send you away when I
become indignant of your stance.

Then come back to me adorned in sheer robes,
layers and layers of cloth wrapped around
your body and around my womb.

Let's wash in innocence,
anoint with new incense.
Use enough perfume to fill
the whole room.

Then you are in a shade closer your hue.

Hallowed Be the Pain

The isolation is still with me.
The parade of daily pain:
> Give us the daily range
> To assist in our transactions
> Traveling the plain of life,

From the Sea of Enchantment to the
Shores of Tranquility,
through all phases of the moon,
to the governing of my cycles to the
mind that portrays all.

Influence me,
Become me,
Divide me and
Recombine me.

Make me invisible so
> some eyes see me,
> some eyes don't.
> eye see me.

On Craycroft Street

But I want sex, any way I can arrange it.
I want to be able to feel passion drive me.
I want him to touch my breasts because
they ache with sore tenderness.
He sucks them and drinks them clear and
turns me on until I'm in ecstasy all over inside.

Then I lie there letting me feel him
feeling me for a long,
long time afterwards.

I don't know what I'm going to say the
next time he drives down.
I feel this is a crisis.

Oh, shit, just what I need.
I probably won't tell him anything
just like always.
But I need sex.
I need it, need it,
I see myself saying this and
shaking his shoulders.
It's like an addiction.
When I can't have it I suffer.
When I find someone new it's so sweet.
I sit and listen to him speak of what he's done
sexually with another woman.
I think that I would never do
anything like that.

But I do live vicariously through his stories
and I want to *experience* them now. I want to
live those stories, all of them, now
before I discover something amiss.

With you, now, I can't live because you say
you have already lived.
So what do you want me to do,
sit and watch you turn to mold,
to a fungus that dries and
bursts into a fine powder spraying the air
like a just-fired gun?

Thoughts are becoming more painful.
Lucidness is escaping me.
I can't face the real issues.
I see the end coming before anything has even
happened.

Endings are long hauls
that gather more burdens to be shrugged
 off later.
Or else the ending happened a long time ago
and I don't know
what's happening to me now.
I certainly don't know.

Just now, I'm looking at last year, events
around this time,
a day-by-day movie.
Some of the same signs pop up.
I feel the same anger welling up.

Wherever I go, acquaintances, his friends,
bring up occasions,
mention a party last year.
I can't remember if it was before or after
I got that phone call.
Yes, now I remember, it was after,
because I stood and looked at one of his
co-workers and knew she also knew he was
having an affair.
I had told her we weren't getting along well.
She said she hoped times would get better. Her
voice had a sympathetic tone.

I now lean over the chair and stare out the
window at the mountains.
The sunset isn't going to be very pretty
tonight, I think as the last glow of orange is
caught in the swirl of clouds.
The sunsets of late have been so spectacular
that sometimes I wonder what an ordinary
sunset looks like anymore.

Somehow, all this makes me think again of
him, how he is so perfect in so many ways. He
really lives, a fast life before my eyes.
I build him and men like him up in my mind
as masters. I haven't even begun to feel a
master at anything. Besides, right now I only
want sex, in any way I can arrange it.

Loneliness

I'm living one of those lonely nights.
There is no one to share what
I have to give,
No one to give to me.
Sometimes it becomes almost intolerable.

Flashback

You strolled in the darkness of night
and I was waiting at the phone at two a.m.
You see to it that I long for you.
You supervise every time I eat anywhere.
Your dark eyes stare.
You keep me within grasp of strong fingers
and tense muscles.

Even now, years later,
you are a prisoner in my mind.
I thought I was living right now
to the fullest.
But today I realize I'm still waiting
and hoping that you will come
strolling by.

Memories

I live off the floor we made love on.
I live off the wall,
      the light fixture,
      the chair.
I live off the towels that
      rubbed your body,
      your blue jeans,
      underwear.
I live off my fingers
running over your lips,
      your mouth,
      through your hair.

I saw you standing there in the street.
I wished I could have you
Wondered what it would take to get you
      and more,
Instead of having just
the floor and the door.

Today my loneliness is almost gone
But what about my head,
the insides that still hurt?

I wonder as I get another piece of coffeecake.
Am I really running from you?
Am I really gazing at a star
Hoping you will come to rescue me?
Because I'm not getting very far
Gazing at a star.

Hard Times

When the times is bad
I find me a man
and give him all the loving I can.

When the hurtin' is bad
and they tell me my livin' is sin
I sit there all grim
until the next sun begins.

When you go choosing your sides
and placing your bets
        about hard times
        that keep hovering on the rim.

Remember to believe
        about the good times
        that will be settling in.

I hurt so bad.
Where is my lover man?
Come to me.
Come right near me
once again.

The Strength of My Drive

Guilt.
Remove it from sex.
Anything sexual you do is all right.
Go where it takes you,
follow it into elevators,
see it over a cocktail,
find it taking a walk.

Sensual Pleasures.
I please you to please me.
Delights and possibilities open wider
until I want to come along
home with you.

Sensual Pleasures.
Endless opportunities with a
sex drive that is insatiable,
I discover.

If you are not here when I want you,
I scream.
I go into fits of starvation and withdrawal.

I know no matter how often I make love
and with the greatest passion,
no matter how great it is, sooner or later the
desire comes creeping back.

I am as certain as the moon grows larger and
larger, moving across the sky, spilling over
full, emptying out, to start all over again.

My Itinerant Lover

My itinerant lover comes
and goes at will.
I cannot stop him, clutching him, pleading
that he needs to rest awhile longer.
However, he comes and goes
with consistent regularity.
When he leaves I swear
I never want to see him again.
But he always comes back when
I want him most strongly.
I begin to count the days;
I doubt if he does.

How does he decide, my itinerant lover,
Just making the rounds of women, forgetting
about me completely
until one day some passion stirs.
I do not know.
Did he pass me from a distance?
Did some other woman remind him of me?
I do not know.

One day he will suddenly appear, insolent,
bearing a mood I haven't seen before.
My guess isn't part of a test,
but he sure knows to pick the spot that incurs
my wrath.

The Forever People

I tread water in your blue swimming pool.
I face the corner of the whitewashed brick wall
built high enough to keep out nosy neighbors,
built high enough to keep out the rest of the
world.

Above, the blue sky crossed with electrical
wires,
          birds line up.

Here I am high on eternity,
soaking it all in with my eyes closed
floating on my back.

It was your eternity, too.
As I sneaked in the back
when you were not looking
I didn't want to take too much,
so you wouldn't miss eternity
the next time you swam in your pool.

Exasperation

Scientific Study Says Greater Math Ability
in Boys vs. Girls

What am I to do?
I have a male mind
inside a female body.

No switching pants,
no sex changes, please,
no alternatives will change the real facts.

No amount of scientific study
will change what I have known from
childhood.

Really, I'm one step ahead of science.
Men actually feed their minds
from their crotch
and I have never suffered that disadvantage.

How Did I Know?

How did I know?
I knew by the way you
crossed your heart.
I carved out a piece with
a hammer and chisel
and placed it on a platter made of steel.

I shouldn't have thought you could take me
seriously.
I should have known that my task is the same
as the woman one hundred
years before me.
I should have figured out sooner
because I walked your streets,
I drank from your faucet, handled your keys
and started your car.

Now reports come in that I told the secrets of
your soul to a man on the streets posing as one
who knows.
He took me in a sentence worth of words.

I said I'm only in between jobs
and I laugh at life
knowing who really told.

Part II

Fireflies as Alibis

On Wings of Poems

I am wicked,
I am bewitched,
I am carnal,
I am woman
        who knows the hearth, the exact spot,
upon which the Earth was born
by a woman's brew.

Except now the Earth runs scared,
the places deemed to be sacred
are no more.

Scared, see the scars of
        anger and hate
        against each other
        man against man.

        Gashes in the earth
        open pit wounds,
        spastic rocks shake,
        shock waves quake,
        gathering force,
        gathering speed.

        Man, you're running,
        running, racing out of control
        scared to look back,
        afraid to know.

What is to Come

Meditation:
I tossed a handful of sticks to the ground,
played them like jacks.

The sticks are gray and weathered bits of twigs
fallen from the nearby palo verde tree.

>We talk about her life, of course.
>We talk about how much longer she
would stay around now that our love was
found and the falling sticks form a triangle.
>We talk about whether I should change
jobs, if the time has come to lead on my own
and the sticks fell, one glanced off away from
the rest.
>We talk about the unity of a home and
the source of strength it provided and the
sticks stacked up with the fattest on top.

And the desert floor was sandy and hard,
a good landing for meditation sticks.

What is Essential: Sensual

Oh, I said, the breezes towards night,
that rush up my sides
          push at the light
curl up in my crevices
          make me sigh.

Hurl me up high to
        float on its cushion of air,
.Dip down into my pores,
        blow away all sores.
Mind you, I say, be wary of battling against
storms. Listen to the winds:
        "Wind Whispers a Seamy Tale."
        Rustling, whistling, wheezing, passing
in and out, touching on all,

        But alas, at last drops to rest.
        Asleep.
Dreamy eyes, stop your sighs.
What, with the advent of a new breeze,
You can open your sides, stand broadside,
facing the gale.

Dreamy eyes, now blow out the candles.
Sun has set. Darkness awaits nearby.

Wait! Sh hh hh hh. I'm catching fireflies
to wear as alibis and then please leave me
sway with the wind.

This Phase of the Moon

This phase of the moon has come around once
again so soon,
this phase of the moon.

Last time I saw you dark and in gloom,
wondering if you'd ever come
back to my room,
this phase of the moon.

After all the time we've spent knowing each
other, it would seem we'd be a bit closer
together, this phase of the moon.

One time back I slipped and coasted down your
crescent and landed in this room.
I closed the drapes to shut you out.
I didn't want to see you for a long while.

Meanwhile I sipped sherry and waited for him
to smile.
We tossed around in the sheets,
like a tug-o-war,
tearing apart pillows, feathers carpeting
the floor in fluff,
a grand old rage within these four corners.

Try as I may, I could not loosen the clasp
to let fall my gown.
Down.
It seems the clasp was the shape
of a half moon with points that pricked.
I had to vow to open the curtains soon,
after the half moon.
I had to turn to him and say, I'm sorry
my blood has not flowed in awhile.
I'm sorry, but it doesn't mean I'm going
to have your child.
Besides, I must go, for tonight the moon
must be nearly full.

I want to be alone,
to pull aside the dark folds,
to let the moon shine fully on me.
This phase of the moon.

Violets are Violent

Colored waters
Colored girls
Colored boys
Are rainbows across the sky
In my ears and in my womb.
In the darkness of the night
Beneath the floorboards in my bedroom.
Between the sheets, atop the pillow
In between my legs
Pulling through my head
And out my mouth
These words I said:
        Violet
        Orange
        Blue
        And red.

Then I went back to become
the rainbow in the sky.
If violence can be buttoned like violets
into a blue to make me sneeze,
there would be the violence of violet.

Some violets are violet, some roses are rose,
but all oranges are orange.

Some roses are red, some violets are blue,
but all oranges are orange.

Some roses are yellow, still all oranges are
orange and all violets are violent.

Hindsight

The temptation is to stay here
all the time,
guarded from the rest of the world,
where my thoughts are my own, undisturbed.

I know.

I'm a dreamer going from star point
to star point,
of worlds that never happen.
I do believe in turning around
and starting again.
I have no feelings about what's
out in the cold.
Sometimes I find myself difficult
to be with
what's here and what's now.

To be a pretty face.

I know I'm not alone, but I don't know
where I'm supposed to be.
The evidence is scattered like
birdseed in the wind.
There is a pattern there, I am assured.
I search and search for dangers of all kinds,
only catch a glimpse of your face as it glanced
off the road.

I believe in magic and embraces in
the middle of the night
          and all that wards off scorn.

I once thought I could have the courage to be
seen and revealed, now I know I can't.

Nevertheless my search continues.

Meanwhile I'm still plastering marmalade to
the corners of my bread,
am back to where my thoughts,
alone, are my own.

The Corn

I suffer from illusions of the mind,
that familiar ring of fantasy:
       I believe in star dust and traveling on
different planes.
       I know each time I feel the clouds pass
through me.

I wonder about the fancies of the stars tonight
and all the trivia we filter through
the sieve of our minds.
I wonder about the holes that are permanent
in my brain from the breezes that blew across
the lake to my perch in a tree.

This I do know for certain:
       as the corn grows the sunlight filters
to the ground,
       when the corn tassels, I ache for the
warm blanket of winds to cover me.

Then the fireflies come out of hiding.

I am sure.

Diversions

I'm saving my money for a plane flight
to the land of make believe.
I'm saving my hair to grow long
to roll in curls for one who loves me.

Some morning I plan to sneak up on him and
he'll awaken to find my heels in his closet, my
perfume on his bathroom counter.

I will make a promise to stop swimming in
pools without lifeguards under the full moon.

Other promises I intend to keep:
      to return to my senses and begin again
      with the new season of flowers,

      to cover the sleeping children and cry
      with the midnight hour,

      to shovel over old rocks and repair the
      path of rainstorms,

      to wonder at the nature of desert rats
      and mockingbirds that never cease
      to sing,

      to carry with me a small book of poems
      to read while waiting for connections of
      the mind,

to begin a new chapter each day,
to cover over dirty words meant only
for dirty minds,

to keep track of statistics so I know to
eat as much ice cream as everyone else,

to think of a good story to tell about
missing my flight,

to say the swallow came swooping
down to pick up the crumbs
and the drums rolled,
          rum-de-dum-dum.

Plenty of visitors gather to hear the story.

None stay for the ending:
They didn't want the illusion to stop.

Departure

Invent yourself.
Define the ways you can circle the yard,
circle the trees, go around the world.

Put yourself in a place where perhaps
only butterflies can land.
Put yourself there now,
far away from here.

Witness yourself flying.
Feel the breeze flowing
through your hair.
The wind brings tears to your eyes.
Let them flow.

You have truly departed from the
ordinary world.
You can see above all of them and underneath
their shirts and behind their sunglasses and
well composed smiles.
You can see clear
through them to the other side.

Happy that you departed.

Disclosure

I went for a walk the other day
And saw the sun rays play.

I was concerned about worldly affairs
and not of the other world.

I happened to see a cloud chasing through the
blue. I happened to hear the wind rustle the
leaves like the rain.

I sighed and collapsed to the ground
and began wondering about the other world.

I didn't want to be deceived by what I saw.

I didn't want to crush the leaves
and make the birds stop singing.
I didn't want to stir up the
dirty bottom of the pond.

I couldn't sit in stillness forever,
because dark comes quickly,
the air chills and makes my teeth chatter.
I was so far away from worldly affairs.

Disclosure II

I spend my days wandering around in the
mystical, rambling around, as one who walks
in the desert and stops to view a rocky vista, or
stoops down to watch a water spider gliding in
a pool reflecting a rainbow on the bottom.

Everywhere sounds the colorings of nature.

I sit and ponder by a gushing falls, listening
to the rapid fire talk with the trees and rushes
and stones. The rocks resist and plow the
stream like a cloak over dark shoulders.

I wish on the ripples as I toss copper pennies
from my mind. Here are the mysteries we all
try to grab and hold in our hands.

I seek to bring the song of the bird through
me. To sing with my eyes closed.
To sing with my heart throbbing with joy.
To hear the melody ring between the
mountains.

I am a bird, strange as it may seem.
I am a bird. I am fanciful.
I flutter around. I bring messages down.
I see other camps.

I fly high just beneath the clouds.
I am winged. I am wonder.
I am free. I am a bird.

Part III

Face the Wind

Backlash

Now I can turn away and say
that poems are just a recording
of mundane days, sultry nights,
seasons of change.

Poems quickly tell of life that has passed
me by, too quickly for me.
I create urgencies to live faster by,
of time switching in dark rooms,
where this moment is all,
where men come to show me they are
guardians of what I am to know Sometime in
the Future, a future, I say, that may never
come around.

I am a woman who knows that the seasons
and time go on and on.
Times were I thought only a Man could do
somewhere in my arms.
Those times are passing, I no longer need to
bewitch and pass the time later guessing
which is which.

Seeing Daylight

Blossoms in the snowdrifts
and cotton in the rain,
Droplets of sap stick to the terrain.
Crushed dew beads and colored water
lurk in all that I dream.

Creamy lakes of lather froth,
burden my soul.

Blatant are the blues.
Quarrelsome are those who
listen to the news.
Who's to blame and who's to lose?

I listened and saw snakes in the aftermath
curling up out of the water.

I thought if I persevered the punishment
would not be so severe,
because I believe in cardinals and other birds
even if I have never heard them sing.

Let me tell you something else:
        I believe in clipping precious roses from
the bush so as to touch and admire them,
        because that is my heart that has been
torn and left for lost in a world forlorn.

I capture a moonbeam to tie shut a present.
I still believe in cardinals and songs of birds
I've never heard.

Thoughts are Words
Without Sound

She kneads his flesh with her fingers,
stops awhile at the pelvic bone.
asks his flesh to speak to her.
Her fingers wonder what it has to say,
what sighs are held within,
what battles are being fought,
whether to yield to this woman who wanted
his flesh to speak or resist
like he did with his woman before
who asked him to speak to her
when she was sad.
He didn't.
Who asked him to speak to her
when she cried; he didn't.

I love you more away than here.
You always want to know my thoughts,
but you might intrude on a moment as now,
look over my shoulder and say,
What silly words you put on paper,
out of time,
no phrasing, jumbles of thoughts.

I'd answer, I'm writing a sensational poem,
bouncing back everything that touches me:
My fern doesn't care if the bedroom door is
opened or closed, because it stays in the
kitchen and lives a contemplative life,
open only to the mysteries of its own
existence and sustenance.

I Don't Feel Naked with My Clothes Off

When I take off my clothes,
I don't feel naked;
most men do.
When I put my clothes back on,
I don't feel dressed;
most men do.

I look at taking clothes off
as a way of thinking,
of wanting to return to a more
natural state of mind,
to be open both inside and out,
so dispense with the clothes.

I see great beauty in the body,
the statuesque folds, lines and curves,
shadows with color.

Why do I need words, when all is revealed
in my body,
my mind?

Endless Night

Sometimes I can't hold onto myself.
When I leave go who will catch me
as I fall?
Who will guide me through the
free fall of space,
>When I know I can't turn back,
>There's no turning around,
>When I know I may never again
>touch ground?

Be as endless as the black night.
Be as remote as one in a dream.
Be as far away as one locked up in tears.

I know I don't want my tears to be
strung in pearls to be worn
around another woman's neck.

The Shadow

The shadow pursued me
covered me like a veil
I was invisible standing behind him,
grey and light as the air of a cat.

Like a shadow he pursued me
covered me with his grey,
so I became a part of him,
part of the air he breathed
and the dust his shoes tracked
in at the door.

One day he scrawled with his fingertips
a message on my skin.
He puckered his lips and
the love flowed in.
I asked, Why do you come to me this way,
unadorned and grey,
when you could be the light,
the dawn of the day?

My naive self still
does finger painting,
writes child stories
about fairies and kings and queens.

I listen.
I hear the sadness of the rocking chair
outside my bedroom door rocking my sister to
sleep. And the sadness flows in like a stream
in the dream I dream.

In Between

I always keep a white man on my left and a
black man on my right.
I always stand in between holding hands.

Sometimes I walk with one and come back
later for the other.
Sometimes I don't see either
for a long time,
Because I change my ways and both are
suddenly black,
or magically white.

I lose touch when they're both the same,
I don't know which is bad and
which is good.
What does it really matter,
when I'm violet in between?

The Barrio

Out in the deep black bottom
buried in the barrio
are the back reaches of my soul.
I see a form emerge briefly
taking on the anger I have stored,
the bitterness that flows from my crevices, the
burden I have stumbled with
ever so long.

All comes crashing down, exploding violently
in the dark reaches of my soul.
Lighting up just enough for me
to see the form taking hold,
pushing and choking its way out.

Tears burn when I drive my car
down the street.
Tears well up when I lay in bed,
awake late at night.

The form stares me in the face,
and turns every which way I go.
A shadow stalking my empty shell,
until I am exhausted and don't
 care anymore.

What promise must I extract from you
to leave me?

Death.

Someday the War
Will Be Over

This is my contribution to ending the war:
      I continue to hoe the garden,
      I continue to tend the cows,
         water them down,
         wander after them up and
         down hills.

At night the soldiers come.
a straggler on the hill,
I take home to love.
The rest of life is taken up in my dreams.
      I hug other women close,
      We hold hands and pray.

Otherwise, the war goes on.
No need to worry about what may
or may not happen.
One day I look at the family jewels,
      finger the pearls,
      diamonds and emeralds
      I squeeze them a few more times
      like rosary beads
      before I take them in for trade.

War stories are great.
Images of desperation, of insanity
eternity in hours, time suspended watching.
Grenades thrown into empty buildings.
only you are inside.

War stories tell of those split second decisions
between life and death,
when you climb the wall and grab onto
whatever crevices will take your fingers
while the explosion takes off the roof and the
floor beneath you.

War stories are great for capturing young men
in the prime of growing awareness of
manhood when they know they can do
anything and certainly will succeed in
conquering the world.

But the enemy will pick you off at the least
suspecting moment.
The children will beg for cigarettes and throw
a grenade in your truck the next moment.

Someday the war will be over.
You will come back to me.
     We'll be that family we so long to be
     with the little table covered
     with a checkered cloth,
     with a sink and running water.

We'll gather around the fire at night to warm
and be cozy before going off to bed.

For now I hold onto other women,
Hug them close,
We hold hands and pray.

Someday the war will be over.
And you will come back to me.
For now soldier kisses, silent meetings
In the middle of the night. Bodies touching.
Energy stored pours from every
muscle and blood vessel.
Parts of me burst, that I never before knew
existed.
            Not much talking,
            It all has been said before, anyway.

Touching each other you calm slowly,
steadily you become all
tenderness in my arms.

Later I cry holding your head on my chest.
I have to think about your leaving,
how I may never have you back.
Like the way you were before
you went off to war.

For now I hold onto other women,
Hug them close,
We hold hands and pray.

More War

There are moments when the blood from other humans
becomes a part of your garb
makes permanent marks on your skin.
Dirt and sweat build layers over your body.

There are the times dying is indistinguishable
from living.
When the other side has been entered and
entertained,
when the words and wars and war stories go
on and on.

I come from the country where
few of the battles were fought.
      I go on with my hoeing
        straight rows down the field.

Was there really ever a war?

Topic of Discussion

Death seems the point of discussion
difficult to broach.

It plagues me.
A concept difficult to grasp,
        why do people die?
        I will die, too?
If this is so, why doesn't everyone end it now
just like that, with the snap of fingers
and not worry anymore?

Which makes me wonder.
Why am I alive?
Because I want to experience the beautiful
and the wonderful.
Let it be my decision
when my life's work is done.
To be not afraid to walk the ways of
serenity and security
        lest I never want to leave,
        leave the Earth, my home.

Sometimes I fear.
I might like living so much
I may never want to die.

Trapped

I want to hear from you.
I thought you left town, I said.

I don't want you to go disappearing again.
I sat there and stuttered.

I wanted to just close the shutters.
I was shivering and shaking.
I left because I saw the door close,
I said.

It actually was closed in my face.
I wanted you to see my body.
I wanted to see what else you could see.
I stopped to pose as a question
I waited for an answer
that never came.

I left and screamed,
clutched my purse, held onto my heart,
rolled down the driveway and out
to continue to play my part.
I responded, I saw the door close,

Trapped II

I want to hear from you.
I thought you left town.
I don't want you to go disappearing on me
again, you said.

I wanted to close the shutters,
I kept shivering and shaking.
that's why I left.

(It closed in my face, actually.)

Now I'm back. I want you to see my body,
I want you to say what else you see.

That's all that matters

Or else.
Or else,
I scatter.
Stop and pose as a question,
wait for an answer that never comes.

Outside again, I scream.
I clutch my purse close to my heart
as I roll out and continue to play my part.

Still Trapped

I want him.
I want an ice cream cone.
I want to reveal myself to the world.
I want to spill the beans
all over the place.
I want daring, I don't want danger.
I want a man to be beside me.
I want him when I call. I want him to make
love to me.
I want the love to flow for the rest
of my life.

I want to stop hanging around
on the fringes.
I want him, dear God, I want him now.

I just want to wrap
him in my arms and tell him
everything is all right.

He will become a beautiful man; I know he's at
the point of blooming now,
I know. Please don't destroy.
Please help me preserve.
Please don't go through what
I lived to get here.
It was not necessary at all.
Please, I don't want to have to start loving
another man ever again.

Years Later

It's hard for me to think about that time because he was so brutal to me. I don't want to bring the memories back to re-experience because those were the center of all the pain, the focus of all the suffering I've ever done. I thought it right for me to carry pain. I thought I should submit to his will because I knew I was still serving God. I knew God loved me. My faith is ever strong because of it. I escaped into that feeling so I didn't have to be in my body. I separated my spirit from my body. That's the way I lived. I hid in the clouds and didn't want to reveal myself to anyone.

He called me some of the worst names imaginable. He constantly threatened to tell others of what I supposedly had done. He put me in compromising situations constantly and I compromised myself. He still beat me. He still threatened me. He said I wasn't capable of succeeding on my own. For every dollar I spent on myself, he spent at least ten on himself. I couldn't stop him. So I cut back on what I gave myself. I punished myself. Now years later, I still feel if I spend money on myself he is watching me and taking a lot more for himself.

Seeing Daylight Again

Blossoms in the snowdrifts
and cotton in the rain.
Droplets of syrup stick to the terrain
crushed dew beads and colored water
lurk in all I dream.

I saw snakes in the aftermath
curling out of the water.
I crushed a moonbeam to tie shut a present.
I thought if I persevered the pain would not be
so severe.
Why do I cry and scream when
pleading is enough?

I bless your words that issue forth
in a strong stream of
bullets that explode on impact
twisting the cells of my brain into other
dimensions.

I believe in clipping precious roses from
the bush to be touched and admired
by a heart that has been torn
in a world lost to the forlorn.

I also believe in cardinals
and songs of birds I have never heard.

Secrets

Innocent and child-like she creeps
up the stairs to the box
with secrets she keeps.
The Whole World looks down,
showing her the turning points in her life,
of her desire to be loved.

Seems lifetimes to spend
putting the family into perspective.
Seems many family memories are buried
in that box.
Deeply buried are the memories I want to
forget most of all.

It's those same memories haunt me now
in ways I can't put into words.

Memories that make me move slowly
and do not allow my joy to show.

Points in Time
That Make Me Cry

There are points in time
that make me cry
without really knowing why.

Sometimes it's for men wo are gods
and women who are goddesses
separated by miles and miles of Unknowing.

Sometimes I sit and mourn each turning
away of a man I thought
was here to stay.
That's another reason to cry.

Always, I hear a voice in wilderness
that echoes louder and louder
calling my name.

I wish I could be loved just the same.
I cry and cry.

Sexist Stories

He probably screwed her in the bottom of the
boat while his brother looked away,
steering on course, peering for land.

The black man on the beach
asked me if I wanted to take a boat ride to
Paradise,
to Paradise Island, that is.

He hustles the passengers, his brother runs the
speedboat.
So he says.

I was sitting on the white sand watching the
para-sailors fly through the pure blue sky,
wondering if I wanted to be out there when I
all I could imagine was being scared standing
on the ramp only inches from lapping waves
that seemed to have a mind of their own,
lapping so closely, while I was helplessly
strapped down waiting for takeoff.

Then the black man came over, asked me
if I wanted a boat ride.
He said he knew I had passion.
I said, You must say that to them all.
No, he said, I see passion in you,
by the way you hold yourself.

He also thought I was from Switzerland.
I thought how lucky he was to have fucked
women from all around the world.
I said it didn't matter whether or not I wanted
to go to Paradise today
because my ship was leaving soon.
There wasn't time enough to get
there and back.

He persisted and took a napkin from a nearby
juice stand,
scrawled out his sister's address where I could
send him
Mail, he said.

Which I never did.
However, on occasion I do wonder about him,
if he's still working that beach, like I'm
wondering now, years later.

Resolve

I have captured the enemy and then let him
go. I question what I will do
with the rest of my days.

Innocence remains.
Sorrows and disappointments are few.

I have extracted myself from many
circumstances, turned over many stones and
left no corners unobserved.
I still carry that hope.
After all else failed, my body remains with me.
It has withstood the battle.

Wearing laurels and ribbons of
triumph in my hair means little.
I picture myself pretty, that's why I smile.
Yet, the torments remain.

My heart is still broken at this time in my life
When I should be at my best.
>   I want to be able to do anything
>   I want.
>   I want the whole world to pass
>   in front of my door.
>   I want everyone to sing with joy.

But my life is not going that way.
How can it be?

> I sit back in reticence.
> I live life half-clothed.
> I don't understand my longings.
> I worry about many matters.
> I live a life of melancholy,
> gravitating between living only in
> a dream.

What is it that will allow me to be happy?
I uncover the rocks and feel the breezes
many times throughout the year.

I comfort the bird with the broken wing
that can no longer sing.

I huddle in the cold outside in the dark
though the fire is warm nearby.

The grass fire spreads,
smoke swirls up in volumes.

The corn burns to a crisp
never to be eaten.

I blow out the flame and
whisper good night.

The Dove Waits

Her vision of this world narrows.
The dimensions become pliable.
Her soul becomes clearer.
The dove waits.

Julie Noterman

Afterward

Though the poems were written years ago, the title is recent. Five years ago I began sorting through my collection of poems, looking for a possible theme, a chronology. All along my reason for writing had been based solely on what I was moved by at the moment, so the subject matter varied widely.

Three years ago I came up with the title "The Waiting Dove" taken from the last poem "The Dove Waits." That title had a quasi-mystical ring, as doves have many symbolic meanings -- one relating to purification of the soul. In my own way I was probably seeking a clear-cut resolution or answer to the experiences of my life, as if there really is an answer. I was also attached to the subject of the poem, an elderly bedridden woman, during her last days alive. We took to each other. In her witty way, she told me that when she no longer had a commentary on someone or something, that would be the day she died. I noticed when that day came and managed to gently forewarn her son, her caretaker, who seemed to think she would live forever, against all odds. The answer was clear for me watching her, as clear as I want my life to be for me.

Nonetheless, from the image of a bird came a form to wrap the poems around. The poems shaped into three parts of a bird in a progressive movement from the left wing, to the body or belly, to the right wing. Parts I, II and III.

The present title "Bloodletting" is in reference to a recent skirmish with the National Endowment for the Arts by those who are squeamish about what is art. I'm referring to a performance art piece funded in 1994, which involved making another actor bleed onstage, the real stuff, not like in the movies. Somehow this performance became characterized by the word "bloodletting." I like that, the way of applying a clinical term to remove oneself emotionally from the impact of the subject matter, the controversy.

I thought, how appropriate for a book title, that poems about the pleasures and pains of love and sex will make some people squirm. In fact, my computer search turned up four references to blood in my poems. *Bloodletting* adds two more as it then became necessary to give that title to a poem. The poem was really written around 1973, but because the title is apt for today, it is the only poem in which I took the liberty of updating the title.

In releasing these poems to the public I run the risk of feeding the myths of the 1970s, the era in which I entered adulthood. Most of the poems were written in that decade. My life latched onto the wave that swept much of my generation, bent on changing a worn-out past with a fresh spirit of freedom, experimentation and questioning all that we had. The danger for me now would be to succumb to recreating that past in my life for the sake of the reader, especially since my writing is not the same today.

However, what I stand to gain is the possibility for other women to begin to heal wounds from relationships, intimate relationships. And it takes a long time, I know. This is my chance to give back.

Now in the 1990s, much of the spirit of the 1970s has passed, but little has changed in the behavior between men nd women. Look at the trial of the century that goes on today, the O.J. Simpson murder trial. The accused is charged with taking abuse to the point of murdering his ex-wife. I am reminded that every woman does not make it out safely. I was lucky. I survived.

My wish and hope, if all else fails, is that these poems serve women well -- serve men, too, to challenge their thinking, to get to know themselves and their women on much deeper levels.

Julie Noterman